Dear Parent,

This **Fun To Do Book** consists of four chapters. All are important to your child's having a happy time in school! If your child is successful in school in the first grade, the chances are he will continue to be successful! He will enjoy his early school experiences! He will feel proud of what he already has learned! He will be able to "build upon" the learnings which he has developed with YOUR HELP! Then he will feel good about himself.

The chapters are:
1. **All About Me**
2. **Fun With Colors and Shapes**
3. **Numbers for You**
4. **A Parade of Letters**

All of these are areas of learning that you can teach your child! He needs this help from you! With patience and understanding on your part you can help your child HAVE FUN and LEARN at the same time!

But your child needs you when you are in a happy mood yourself, when you feel like giving words of encouragement and praise, and when your child is READY!

I wish you much success in working with your child.

Happy teaching!

Ruth Bowdoin

THE BOWDOIN METHOD

1. All About Me

This chapter is designed to help your child understand the parts of the body. Would you believe that this is important to your child? Yes! As a child has experience in seeing the relationship of one part to another, he will become aware of himself in his environment. This is important to the beginning of the development of other motor skills. As a child becomes aware of self, independence develops.

Your child needs. To point to his own eyes, nose, hands, ears, arms, legs, head, hair.

• To wash and dry his hands and take care of his toilet needs.

• To learn the front and back of clothing as he learns to dress himself.

This chapter is important also because it will help your child learn to appreciate and like himself! This certainly has much to do with ability to learn.

Read this chapter many times! Point out the body parts.

I have a pretty round face,
and I have hair on top of my head.
Sometimes it grows long
and tickles my face!

And two eyes
that see many pretty things.
Animals on the farm.
Birds in the treetops high.
Squirrels eating a nut.

I have one nose
but it can smell many things...
clean clothes in the sunshine,
cookies baking in the oven,
flowers growing in the yard,
perfume that my sister wears!

And I have a mouth!
Sometimes it eats.
Sometimes it talks.
Sometimes my lips poke out!
But I'm not pretty that way.
When I am happy, my mouth says so!
So I just smile and smile and smile!

I have two ears
on the sides of my head.
Listen! I can hear something.
I hear many nice sounds —
My mother singing,
the bell ringing,
the bees buzzing,
my granny laughing,
the kitten mewing,
the dog barking!
I hear nice sounds with my ears.

Do you see my neck?
What does it do?
It holds up my head.
It helps it turn from side to side.
My shoulders are wide and grow from my neck.
I have a nice neck and big, big shoulders!

Up and down!
Up and down!
I can move my two arms around
and around!
They can throw balls.
And hug my mother!
I have four fingers and one thumb.
One, two, three, four, five!
They help me color and draw,
and play!

I have a body.
It bends.
And moves.
And sits.
And stands!
And my two legs
walk and skip and jump!

I have two feet.
They have heels and toes!
One, two, three, four, five
toes
on each foot.

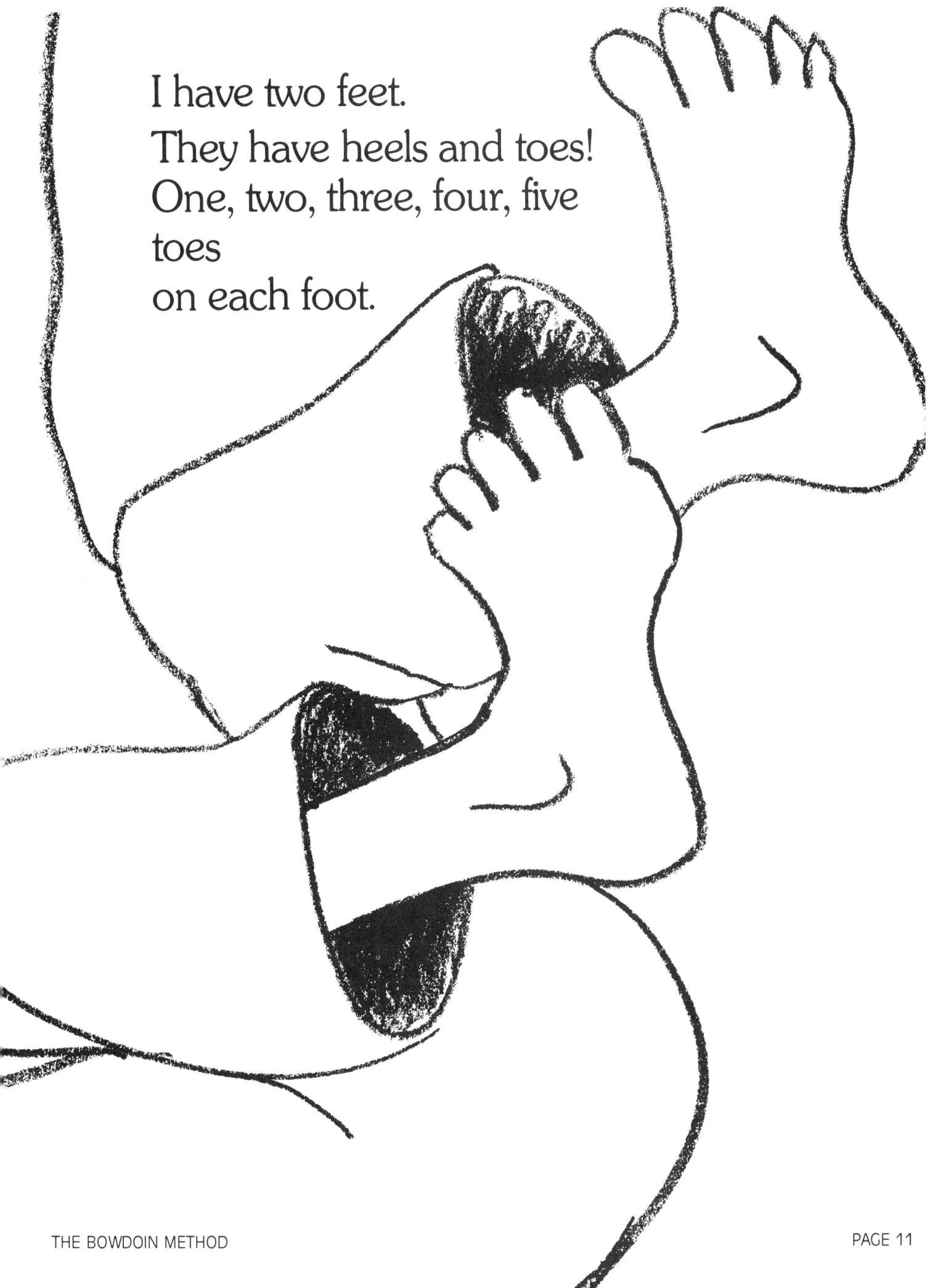

2. Fun With Colors And Shapes

Read this chapter many times to your child. He will be learning shapes and colors. He will be learning to think, to imagine! How good he will feel about himself when he enters first grade! It takes much repetition and much PRAISE before your child learns colors and shapes.

Remember, children need to know *thousands* of word meanings. There are more than 200 in this chapter. Your child will learn the meanings if you read to him.

You may wish to encourage your older children to read to your smaller child. They may enjoy it, too! MAKE IT FUN!

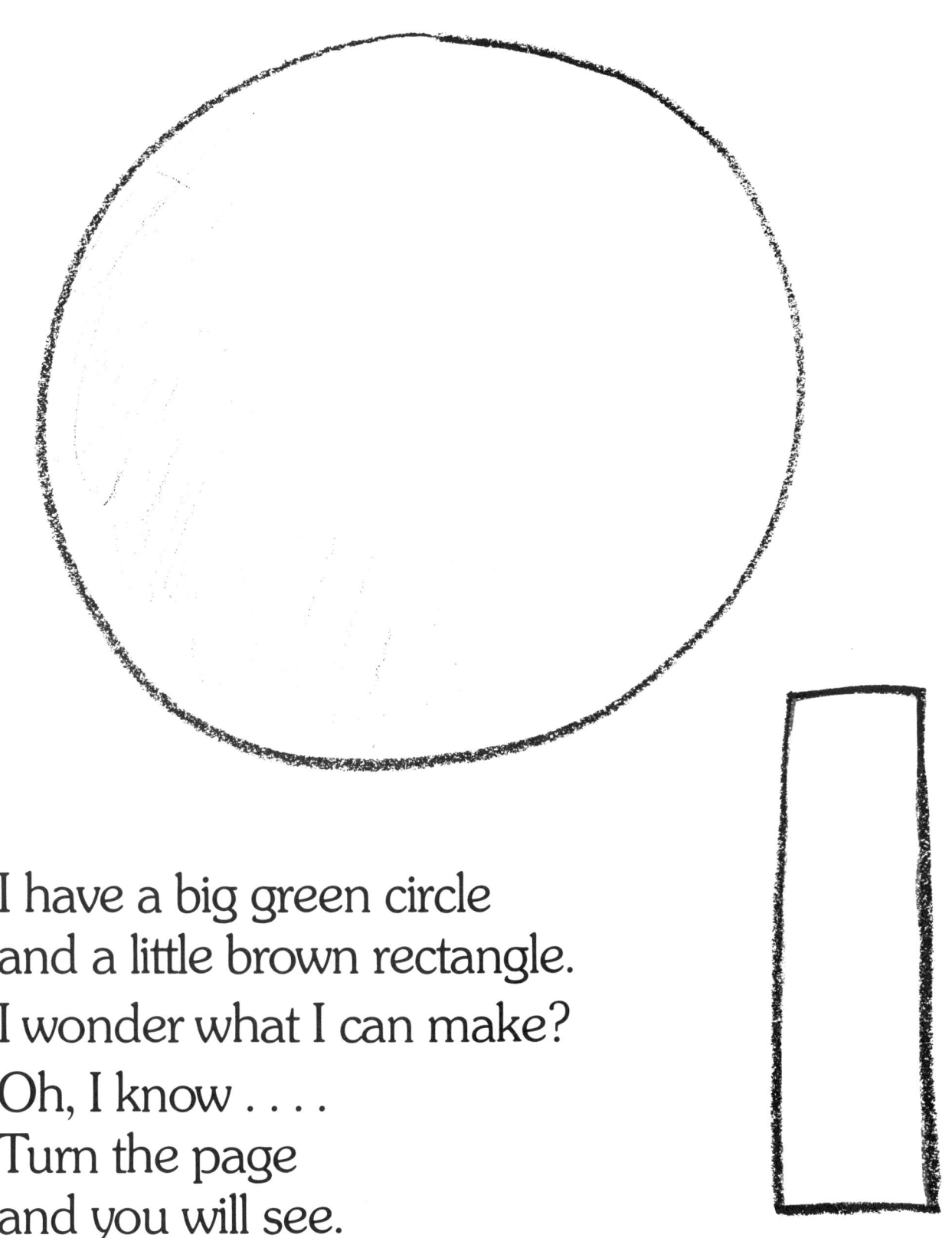

I have a big green circle
and a little brown rectangle.
I wonder what I can make?
Oh, I know . . . .
Turn the page
and you will see.

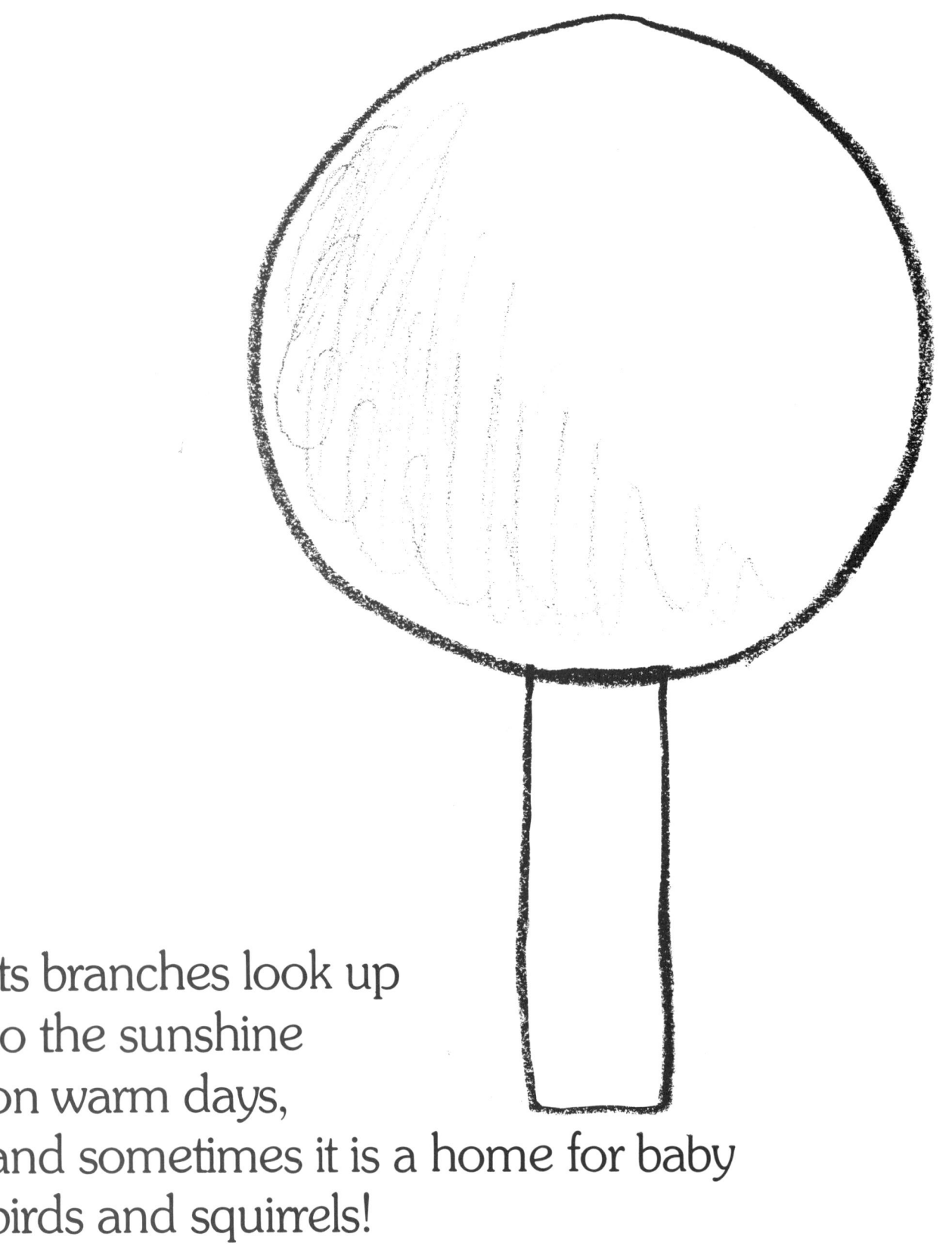

Its branches look up
to the sunshine
on warm days,
and sometimes it is a home for baby
birds and squirrels!
What a nice tree I made!

Here are lots of shapes—
a small black rectangle and
a small black square.

Also, one, two, three, four big squares that are
blue, yellow, green, and red!

And one, two, three, four, five, six,
seven, eight brown circles!

What can I do with these?

Let me think.

This is difficult. Oh, I know. . . .

Toot! Toot!
I made a choo-choo train!
Here I come, clickety-clack, clickety-clack!
The wheels go round and round.
The engineer blows his whistle.
I like my train!
Do you know the colors of my coaches?

I have some shapes to play with—
a black square and
three white circles,
a little circle,
a bigger circle,
and a great big circle.
I wonder what I can make?
Oh, I know. . . .

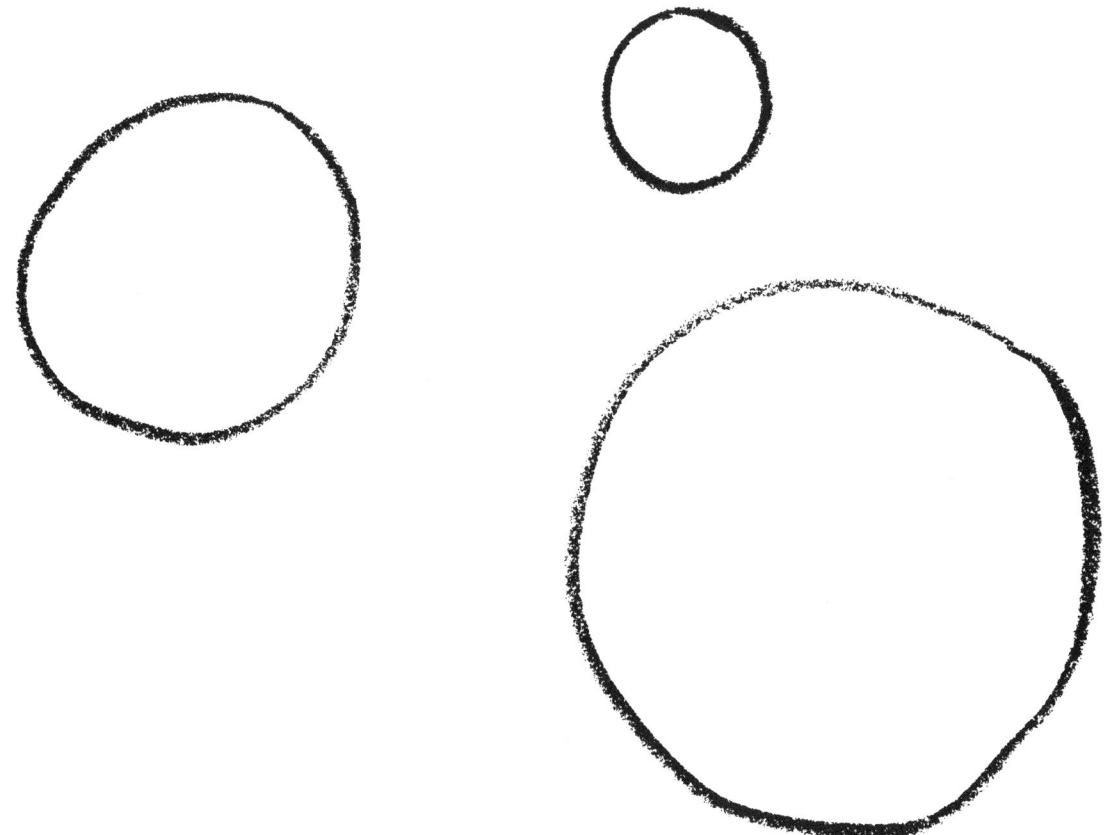

Why, yes, of course!
A snowman!
I made a snowman with three white circles.
The black square is his hat.
I made a broom beside him.
I put a red scarf around his neck.
I made a happy snowman!
Happy, happy snowman!

What shapes do I have here?

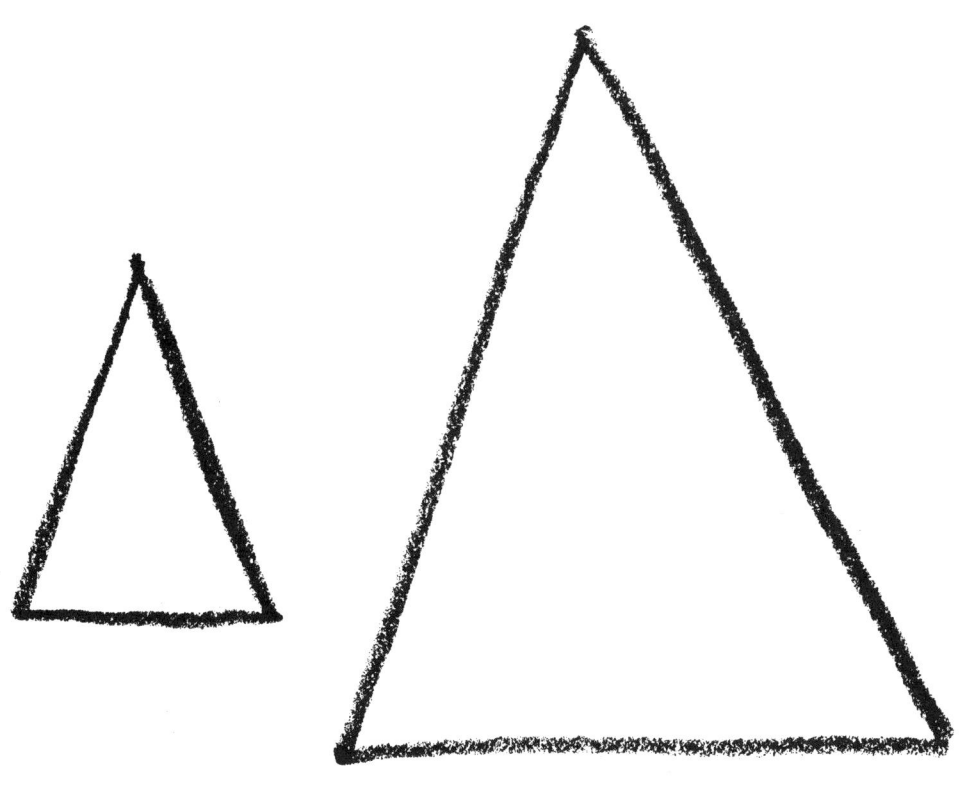

I have one small, yellow triangle.
I have one big orange triangle.
I have two brown lines.

I wonder what I can make.
Oh, I think I know. . . .

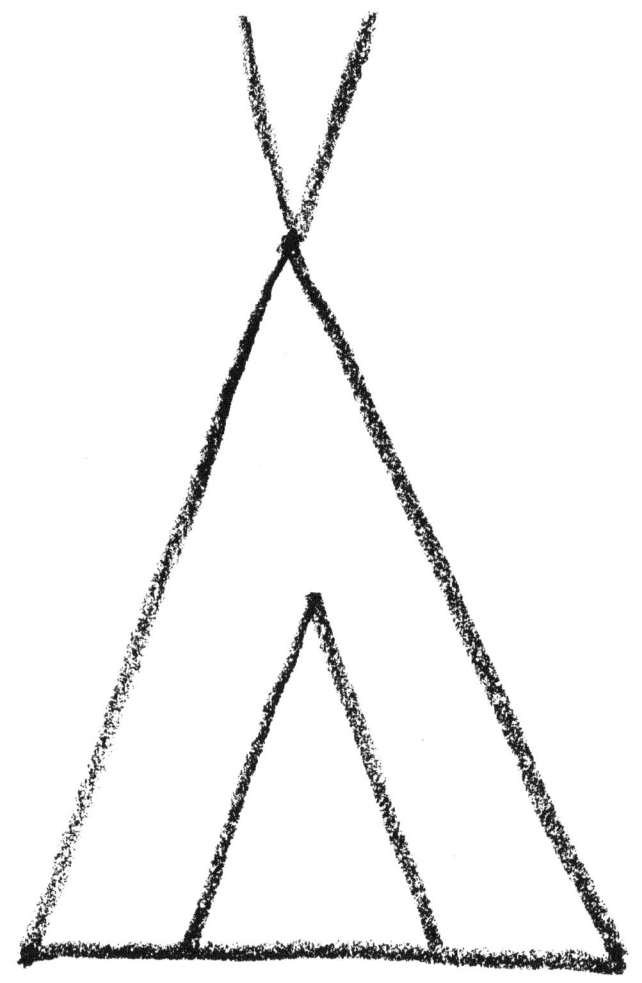

See what I have made — a teepee!
My teepee is the big, orange triangle.
The door to my teepee is the small, yellow triangle.
And the two brown lines are the top of the Indian house.
What a nice teepee I have made with my shapes!

I have more pretty shapes —

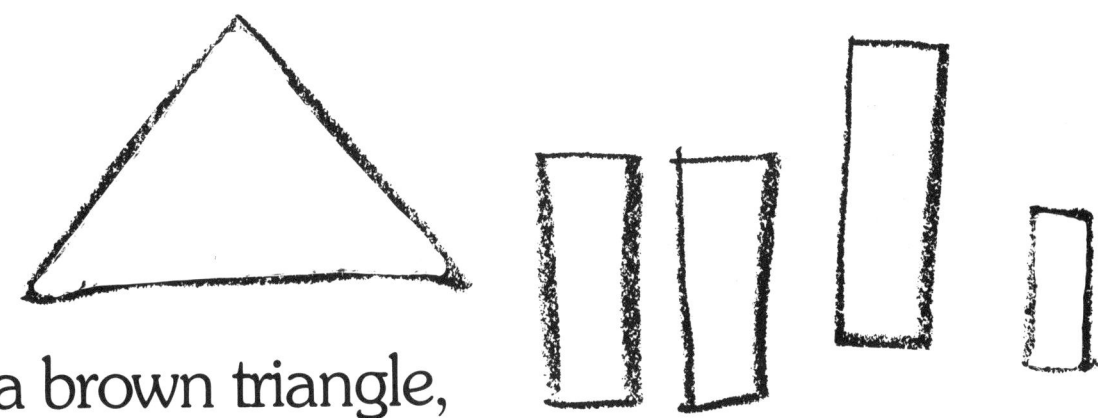

a brown triangle,
two small yellow rectangles,
one long yellow rectangle,
one small red rectangle, and

a large green square.
Now, what can I make with these?
I know.

I can make a house—
A little green house
with yellow doors and windows
and a red chimney on top of the
brown roof. I like my little house.
Does a nice family live inside
my little house? Yes, a mother
and some children and perhaps a daddy.
It is a happy house!

What do I have here?
I have a yellow star;
one, two, three, four, five.
six red circles;
a green triangle; and
a brown square.
If I put on my "thinking cap,"

I can make something.
Oh, I know. . . .

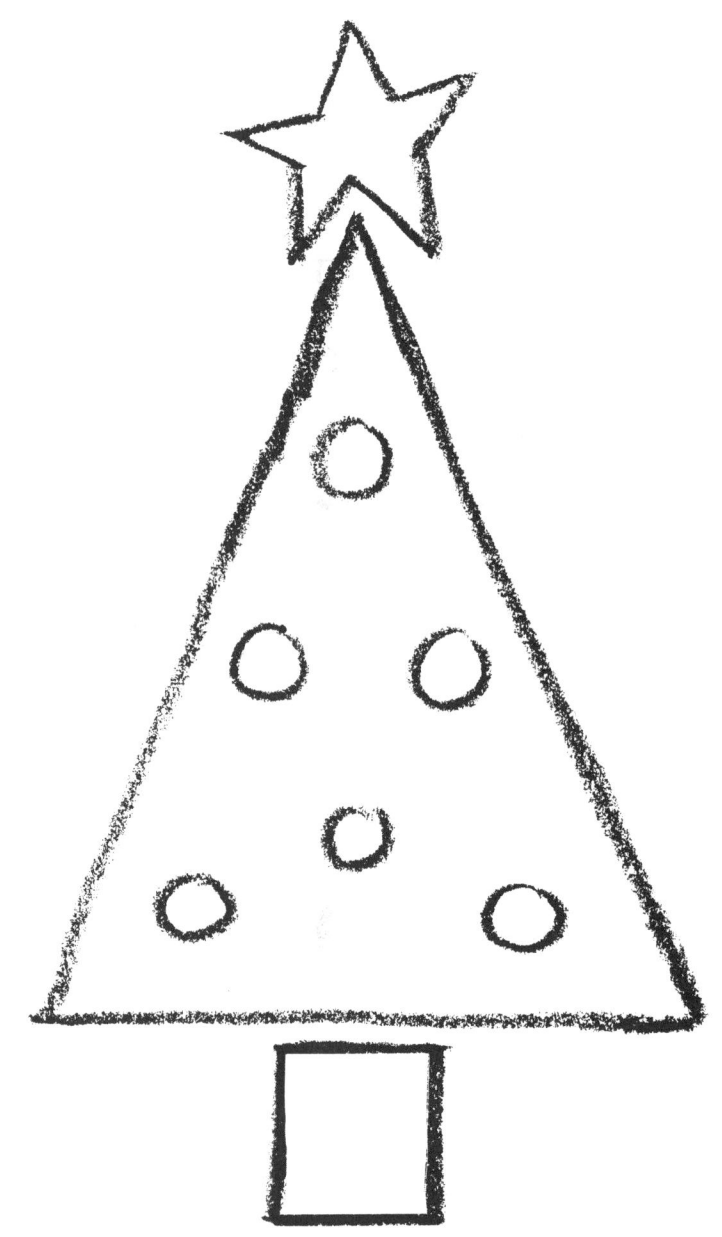

A pretty little Christmas tree I made—
with the red balls for decoration
and a pretty star high up on top.
I like my Christmas tree.
Do you like it, too?

What shapes are here?
There are two yellow hearts,
a green rectangle,
and two brown lines.

What can I make with these shapes?
Oh, yes! I know. . . .

I can make a beautiful butterfly!

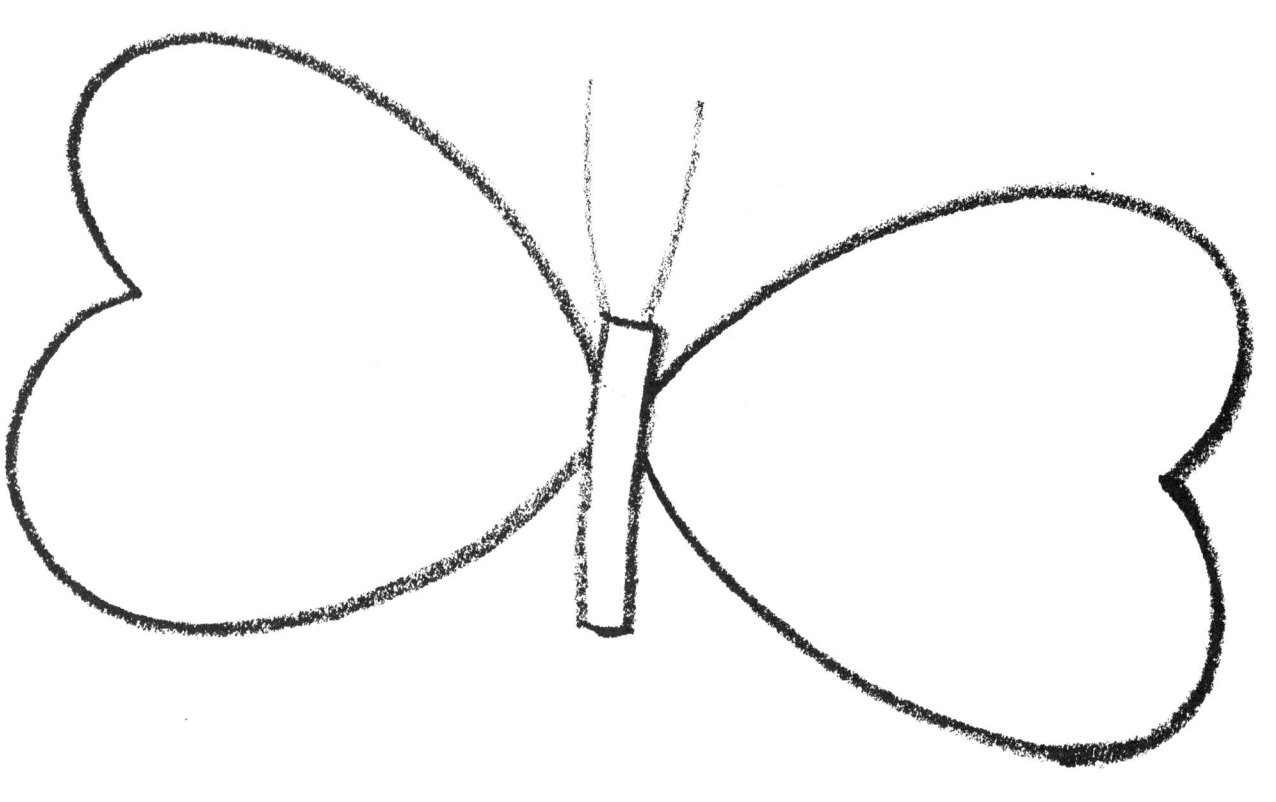

The yellow hearts are its wings.
The green rectangle is its body.
The two brown lines are its "feelers."
See what a beautiful butterfly
I have made with my shapes!

See my five pretty purple circles.
And I have a small yellow circle and a green line.
Let me decide what I can make.

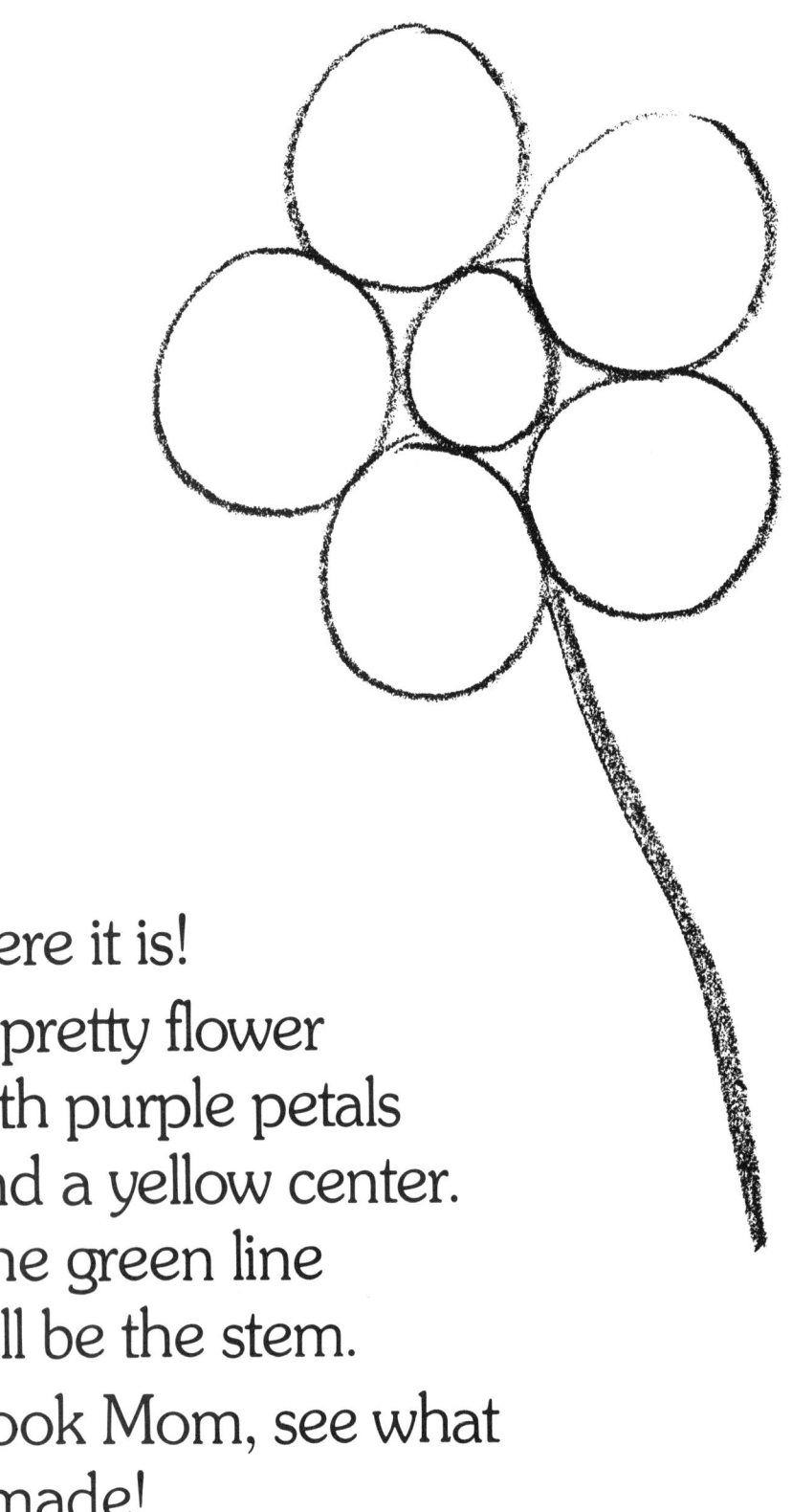

Here it is!
A pretty flower
with purple petals
and a yellow center.
The green line
will be the stem.

Look Mom, see what
I made!

3. Numbers For You

This chapter has been made especially for you! It was made to help you with your child as he learns number meanings and understandings.

Let your child count the pictures on each page as you read the rhymes.

Later on, as your child develops, he may ask what the numerals are. If he does, tell him, but *don't push too fast* by trying to teach these before your child is ready. The important thing is to *teach understandings* of what the numerals really mean.

There are many other things you may do to help your child get ready for formal instruction in arithmetic!

Talk about time — time to eat, time to sleep, time to play. (This will help him understand about time.)

Let your child do simple things, such as counting the number of plates at the table, the number of people in the room, how many chairs we need.

Talk about *big* and *little*, *large* and *small*. Use cans when you are cooking. Ask your child to give you the *biggest* can, the *smallest*, the can on the *bottom* shelf, the *top* shelf.

Talk about *many* and *few*, *left* and *right*, *over* and *under*, *above* and *below*. This will help develop understandings he will need later.

Talk about different shapes — circle, square, triangle, heart, rectangle. Let your child find things in the house that have different shapes.

One big ball
 so nice and **round!**

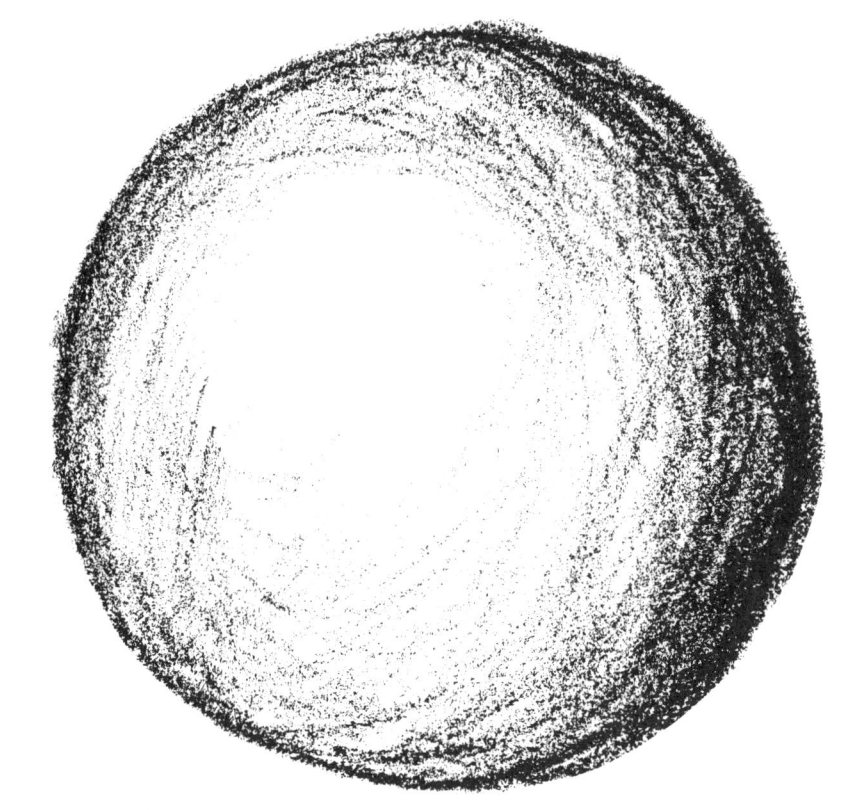

Two red apples
 on the **ground!**

3 Three big drums go . . .
Boom! Boom! **Boom!**

4 Four little kittens
in a **room!**

5 Five flying kites up in the **sky!**

6 Six little bluebirds flying **high!**

7 Seven glowing candles on the **cake!**

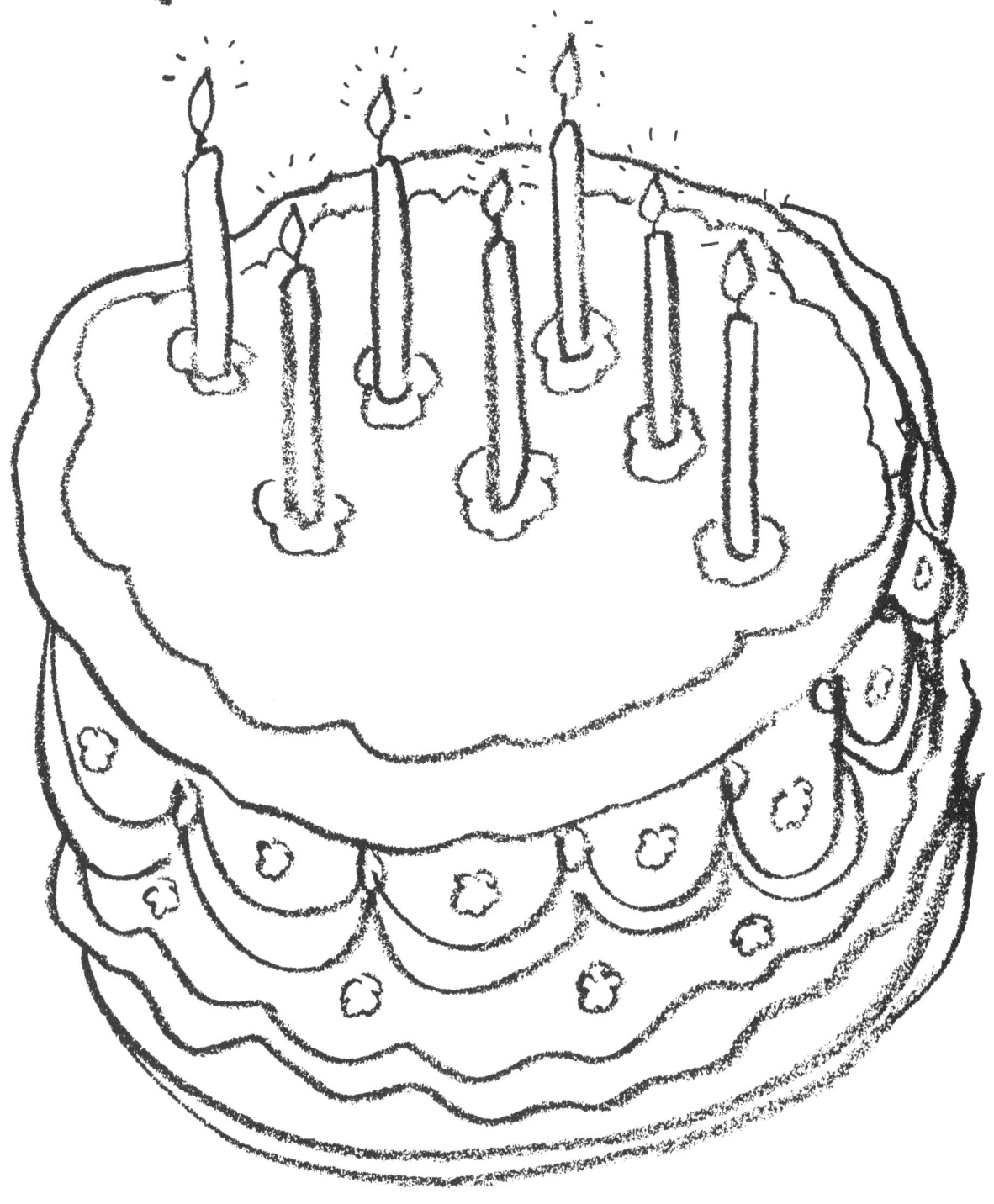

8 Eight steamships upon the **lake!**

THE BOWDOIN METHOD

9
Nine little fish swimming in the **sea!**

THE BOWDOIN METHOD PAGE 39

10 Ten shining stars twinkling down at **me!**

Count these pictures.
See how far you can count.

4. A Parade Of Letters

Studies show that children who know the letters of the alphabet by sight will usually do better when they begin to read.

This chapter will be useful to you to help teach your child the names of the letters. (*But this is not the most important thing you can do for your child. Reading to him and helping him learn to talk in complete sentences and to understand what words say are more important to your child than learning his letters!*)

Sing the Alphabet Song. You will know the tune. If you don't remember it an older child in the family will help, or you may learn it from the Sesame Street program.

It is important that your child learns to recognize these *when he is ready.* But PLEASE, JUST A FEW AT A TIME... AND *ONLY* IF HE IS INTERESTED. YOU MAY DO MORE HARM THAN GOOD IF YOU PUSH YOUR CHILD!

Turn the pages as you sing and point to the letters as you go along. You may be surprised how many your child can learn. Show him the difference in the capital and the small letters.

Praise your child! *Make learning fun* and happiness for your little one.

The Alphabet Song: "A B C D E F G... H I J K L M N O P... Q R S and T U V... W X and Y and Z... I'm as happy as can be... Now I know my A B C's."

THE BOWDOIN METHOD PAGE 43

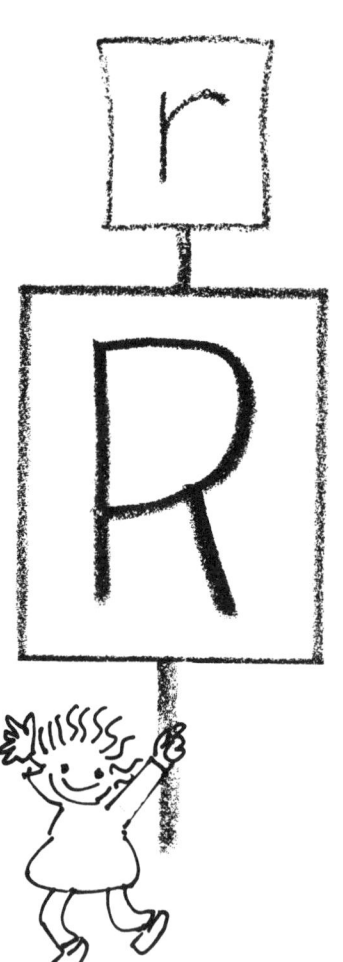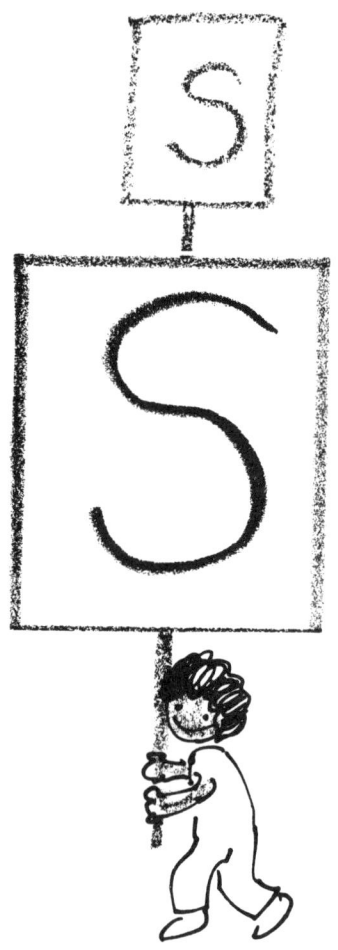

I'm as happy as can be...
Now I know my A B C's.